Timeless

Abigail Sanchez

To all those who have ever felt alone: I see you

PART ONE

SUN AND MOON

SUNSET

I wander alone in this land
No one tells you about this
They expect you to make a stand
No one tells you about this

Worshipers of Misery come to me
Everyone closes their eyes
I'm trying to flee
Everyone closes their eyes

Sunset is coming
Caught in a net
Singing and humming
Filled with regret

How did it come to be?
Nobody hears me running
I beg and I plea
Nobody hears me running

The temple doors are shutting
The rope around me is binding
The bluebells they are cutting
And mashing and grinding

* * *

Twelve petals pass through pale lips
Everything is becoming shattered
My heart becomes eclipsed
And the face turns haggard

Sunset is coming
All the colors in the sky
The heart is thrumming
They turn a blind eye

DUSK

Sunset is coming
All the colors in the sky
The heart is thrumming
I turn a blind eye

How could I ever tell?
This secret that kills me
"Tu est belle"
I'd rather be a flea

It's time for dusk
Eyes are closed
Skin turns to a husk
They pollute unopposed

How could I ever tell?
Medusa cries and screams
In this cave, we dwell
Medusa laughs and dreams

Eyes are closed
It's time for dusk
Lily White stands composed
Lily White is stuck

* * *

Voices in the mind
Point out every mistake
Every flaw is assigned
To every heartbreak

How could I ever tell?
When nobody hears
Ring the bell
But nobody hears

TWILIGHT

How could I ever tell?
When nobody hears
Ring the bell
Somebody hears

Laughing and playing
I see her
Dancing and swaying
So full of mirth

We watched Twilight
She loved it
Innocent and bright
Life-changing, I admit

Do not die for her
Tears will come
Live for her
Thy will be done

She was only four
And saved a life
For her, I'll ignore
And put down the knife

* * *

We watched the twilight
She cannot wait
Starlight, star-bright
Ready to change fate

Do not die for her
She was only four
Live for her
She gave me so much more

EVENING

Do not die for her
She was only four
Live for her
She gave me so much more

Second chances can be given
At the altar, I confess
All is forgiven
I am changed and blessed

It is evening
He gives me life
She gives meaning
And all is right

I am Lazarus
Alive again
From under the surface
And out of the den

It is evening
Irises grow
There is no grieving
Not when I know

* * *

He gives me life
She gives meaning
All is right
All is redeeming

I am Paul
Transformed in faith
No longer called Saul
No longer afraid

10 PM

I am Paul
Transformed in faith
No longer called Saul
No longer afraid

Yet, always a yet
I can never escape
Escape from this threat
That only changes shape

Where are You?
I ask and I yell
For the darkness grew
In my heart, it dwells

Keep the faith
It strangles and chokes
Keep the faith
I become smoke

Daisies are growing
Purple hyacinths are ready
Bluebirds are glowing
The black dog holds steady

* * *

10 pm, I see the night
A road of darkness ahead
There is no end in sight
And so I walk with dread

Keep the faith
They chant and sing
Keep the faith
I cry and scream

MIDNIGHT

Keep the faith
They chant and sing
Keep the faith
I chant and sing

This family by blood
Listen and misunderstand
The bond is a flower bud
Small yet grand

This family by choice
Listen and misunderstand
They hear a passive voice
But this is no fairyland

Tears are shed at midnight
Blood is spilled in the dark
With this, I try to ignite
A dying, broken heart

There is light in the day
There is a mask unassuming
I kneel and I pray
My face bright and blooming

* * *

"Forgive us our trespasses
As we forgive those --"
I look at the masses
I cannot oppose

Midnight is here
The mask is off
Tears appear
It's time for a send-off

2 AM

Midnight is here
The mask is off
Tears appear
This is my send-off

The yellow chrysanthemum
Grows and grows
There is no yellow sun
And time begins to slow

2 am, the end is near
Nothing feels right
Please, somebody hear
This cry in the night

2 am, make a choice
Which is truly worse?
Don't make a noise
This is my curse

2 am, I survive
How can it be?
I counted to five
Am I free?

* * *

Alone in this cave
Screams echo
Wave after wave
A dying, dry meadow

One last chance
To be in the sun
I try to sing and dance
I try to walk and run

WITCHING HOUR

One last chance
To be in the sun
I sing and dance
I walk and run

The witching hour
Fills with fear
The witching hour
I hold dear

Darkness is my friend
Darkness is their enemy
Darkness is not the end
Darkness is serenity

God is not here
For when I plead
He did not appear
He did not free

I survived the night
I opened the cage
I burned bright
I fought and raged

* * *

The witching hour
Fills with fear
The witching hour
I hold tight and near

My heart's delight
My heart's golden lines
I am my own knight
Fighting against my monster's design

FALSE DAWN

My heart's delight
My heart's golden lines
I am my own knight
Fighting against my monster's design

There is a voice
Everyone hears
I make a choice
No more fears

No more false dawns
No more dark years
I right my wrongs
Put away the spears

This is my deliverance
This is my coming home
This is the difference
Of my mind and soul

Yet, always a yet
Bluebells fully grown
Bluebells are a threat
I am again alone

* * *

This is a false dawn
This is a dark year
Cannot carry on
Cannot disappear

Gather strength
I look at the sky
Gather strength
Never say goodbye

DAWN

Gather strength
I look at the sky
Gather strength
Never say goodbye

It's time for dawn
There is one goodbye
In the lake, a swan
Ready to fly high

It's time for a new chapter
There is one goodbye
The swan escapes its captor
And takes to the sky

She soars like never before
There is one last goodbye
At the end of this war
Where there is no lie

No lie of darkness
Just this last goodbye
No lie of the heartless
Just this last goodbye

* * *

It's time for dawn
Say the goodbyes
Free is the swan
To stand and arise

Arise from the darkness
From all that weakens
Arise from the harshness
Of those dark demons

SUNRISE

Arise from the darkness
From all that weakens
Arise from the harshness
Of those dark demons

Sunrise is coming
Let go of the regret
My heart is thrumming
Of things to be said

Yellow daisies bloom and die
But always bloom again
The white dove will continue to fly
Over the valley, it'll reign

Gratitude to the Bluebells
For always shading me
Now I must stand and tell
Tell them to give me the key

My life is my own
My heart is mine
My mind is my own
My soul is mine

* * *

Sunrise is coming
There will be a sunset
But nothing too numbing
I am released from the net

I wander around in this land
I tell others about this
I make my stand
I will tell others about this

PART TWO

HOURGLASS

DARKNESS

Thank you for this
The time you give
To reminisce
And to forgive

It began with her
She was beautiful
Smelled of myrrh
Reputation irrefutable

In love was she
With a man of heart
Both filled with glee
Ready for their start

Then came he
A man of resentment
Filled with jealousy
Showed his discontentment

Reputation ruined
No longer wanted
All disillusioned
And she haunted

* * *

Then came he
A man of stone
Trigger-happy
With a backbone

No choice to make
So she married him
Married a snake
Her face grim

Her love regretted
Forsaking her
But she is wedded
No escape can occur

Purple and blue
Was her skin
No joy she knew
Her heart shut-in

What is left?
Her children wonder
Unloved and oppressed
Even when he is six feet under

SUN AND MOON

What is left?
Her children wonder
Unloved and oppressed
Even when he is six feet under

Alone now is she
With children to care
No degree
No love in the air

She loved the best she could
But only violent love she knew
Taken was her girlhood
But she'll pull through

Daughter's reputation ruined
She tried her best to fix
The situation and
Face society's politics

But the baby girl was loved
Daughter could not give her up
Left her mother stunned
There was no backup

* * *

But Daughter soon left
Left her Mother and Baby Girl
Left them distressed
And away she whirled

Alone now is she
With children to care
With a baby in the family
Oh, how life is unfair

Baby Girl becomes Schoolgirl
Grandmother loves in her way
But even Girl can confirm
They wanted her away

Schoolgirl becomes Young Woman
The hurt continues to fester
Fester in Grandmother and
Mother and Daughter

LIGHT

Schoolgirl becomes Young Woman
The hurt continues to fester
Fester in Grandmother and
Mother and Daughter

Daughter says no more
She stands her ground
She opens the door
New life she found

Daughter is Mother
Mother is Grandmother

But the hurt can stay
Though the mother tries
Her daughter takes the bouquet
Of bluebells of different size

Then Daughter says no more
She stands her ground
The Mother is with her
New life they found

The hurt can fester

Fester in Grandmother and
Mother and Daughter
Until all are shunned

Until there is one
One who says no
One who is done
With the hurt of long ago

Thank you for this
The time you give
To reminisce
And to forgive

NIGHT

It is always night
Everything is alight
Bone-aching
Backbreaking

It is always night
Nothing is alright
Shoulders heavy
Too much to carry

It is always night
They say you're fine
No rest for me
No visit to the sea

It is clear to me
They cannot see
See the weight
See the crate

It is clear to me
I cannot be carefree
My head is pounding
Everything is confounding

* * *

It is clear to me
They cannot agree
On what is wrong
For this illness is long

What is it called?
This disease that crawls
It is not a cold
For it is too bold

What is it called?
This sickness that caused
Such heaviness to exist
Such heaviness to persist

What is it called?
For peace I desire
What is it called?
It is called tired

CLOCK

The mouse runs up the clock
I only stand in shock
Why would they say this?
Why would they dismiss?

I cry and I scream
But to them, I only seem
So spoiled for attention
It is not worth to mention

Do not mention this
The crying and the abyss
Do not try to run
Only because you feel shunned

Can they not see?
I fight to be free
Do they know?
Why I do not glow?

Let me speak
Let me teach
It does not feel bleak
When I give my speech

* * *

Let them know
And let them show
Their love in the snow
Their love in the cookie dough

They are my angels
To protect me from dangers
To see through my behaviors
To block the naysayers

They gave me my name
A purpose to reclaim
There was never shame
We are just the same

I am their miracle

POCKET WATCH

The Rabbit and his pocket watch
The Queen and her hearts
The Hatter with his madness
The girl with her smarts

I and my pocket watch
I and my heart
I with my madness
I with my smarts

The past is past
But lessons are taught
Do not be afraid
Not of this lot

The Rabbit and his pocket watch
The Queen and her hearts
The hatter with his madness
The girl with her smarts

I wish to forget
Let the past be past
And the lessons?
The lessons I passed?

* * *

I and my pocket watch
I and my heart
I with my madness
I with my smarts

Be not afraid
There is much to be taught
There is much to listen
There is much to watch

ANALOG

Maybe this will help
They say, they say
It will help
They try, they try

She is fixed
They say, they say
No more of this
They try, they try

Maybe this will help
I say, I say
It must help
I try, I try

We cannot help
They say, they say
It is too much
They try, they try

I need help
I cry, I cry
Please help
I plea, I plea

* * *

This will help
They say, they say
Sometimes it might not
They try, they try

I try, I try
I cry, I cry
I am not fixed
I am being healed

DAY

I hate you!
I scream and I yell
My life has turned blue
My life has turned hell

I need you!
I scream and I cry
If only I knew
But I never tried

Why did you abandon me?
I cry and I whisper
Am I a fig tree?
Am I a drifter?

There is no God
I say and I say
I feel no awe
I no longer pray

Analog comes into mind
Clock circles my head
These miracles are hard to find
And all this time I've fled

* * *

I learned to trust
The pocket watch
I begin to dust
I begin to wash

Is there a God?
I whisper and whisper
Take off the facade
He whispered and whispered

I need you
I say and I cry
I am here
He says and I cry

HOURGLASS

Worshipers of Misery came to me
Everyone closed their eyes
I really tried to flee
Everyone closed their eyes

Voices in the mind
Pointed out every mistake
Every flaw was assigned
To every heartbreak

It's time for a new chapter
There is one last goodbye
The swan escaped its captor
And took to the sky

Gratitude to the Bluebells
For always shading me
Now I must stand and tell
Tell them to give me the key

The key which unlocks my life
For I no longer need
To arm myself with a knife
It is now time to lead

* * *

Lead my own heart
Lead my own mind
Make my own art
Of my design

The hourglass turns up and down
But now I understand better
Depression may be around
But so is this love letter

ACKNOWLEDGEMENTS

I want to thank everybody who has given me so much support throughout the writing of this book. I also want to give thanks to all those who have been there for me throughout my journey with depression and anxiety.

First, thank you to Dayquan Moeller for helping me edit my poems. Thank you also for advocating for the rights of so many people. You inspire everyone to do better every single day. Keep fighting the good fight.

Second, thank you to my parents for always supporting me. I know I was not always an easy child, but you guys did an amazing job. You helped me realize that I can accomplish anything I put my mind to.

Third, thank you to my big brother and my sister-in-law for your encouragement as I write this book and for making me an aunt to an amazing little boy.

Most of all, thank you to my sister for pushing me to publish this book in the first place and for being my biggest supporter. I could have never done this without you.

www.ingramcontent.com/pod-product-compliance
Lightning Source LLC
Chambersburg PA
CBHW070452130626
46553CB00006B/2382